HELL'S KITCHEN TRASH

I0821402

HELL'S KITCHEN TRASH

RICHARD PANCHYK

America Through Time is an imprint of Fonthill Media LLC
www.through-time.com
office@through-time.com

Published by Arcadia Publishing by arrangement with Fonthill Media LLC
For all general information, please contact Arcadia Publishing:
Telephone: 843-853-2070
Fax: 843-853-0044
E-mail: sales@arcadiapublishing.com
For customer service and orders:
Toll-Free 1-888-313-2665

www.arcadiapublishing.com

First published 2020

Copyright © Richard Panchyk 2020

ISBN 978-1-63499-242-8

All rights reserved. No part of this publication may be reproduced, stored in a retrieval system or transmitted in any form or by any means, electronic, mechanical, photocopying, recording or otherwise, without prior permission in writing from Fonthill Media LLC

Typeset in Gotham
Printed and bound in England

Contents

INTRODUCTION

NEW YORK IS LITERALLY A CITY OF TRASH. New Yorkers throw away an average of 10,000 tons of trash per day. That amounts to over 3.2 million tons of trash per year! That's a lot of garbage, and that does not even include thousands of tons of commercial trash that are hauled away by private carters. Many parts of Manhattan are actually built on garbage—landfill that included everything from pieces of broken ships to bricks and construction debris. Manhattan Island used to be significantly narrower in places, before it was widened with trash. One of the city's most popular attractions, the World's Fair (now Flushing Meadow Corona Park), was constructed on top of a garbage dump. Rikers Island was expanded to double its original size thanks to garbage, and LaGuardia Airport was later built on some of the same trash that was transported from Rikers to Queens.

Trash is all around us, but we've grown so accustomed to it that we may not really notice it anymore. Be prepared, because that may change once you delve into this book.

In *Hell's Kitchen Trash*, we'll take a closer look at garbage—the small and the large, the beautiful and the disgusting, the mundane and the bizarre. The trash in this book is place-specific history, a snapshot of Hell's Kitchen life both past and present, as seen through garbage. It's a photographic history of the discards of several different categories of HK people—its residents, workers, and tourists, all of whom coexist and contribute to the landscape of trash, the many tons of trash generated in Hell's Kitchen every single day.

Hell's Kitchen, located between Eighth Avenue and the Hudson River from roughly 34nd Street (30th Street if you include Hudson Yards) to 57th Street, is an interesting and vibrant location because so many people pass through it on a daily basis, whether they are headed there or their final destination is elsewhere. Hell's Kitchen encompasses two of Manhattan's major transportation hubs—the Port Authority Bus Terminal, and the western end of Penn Station. It also includes the heavily traveled access ramps to the Lincoln Tunnel. The area includes two of the city's most popular destinations: the Jacob K. Javits Convention Center and the Intrepid Sea, Air, and Space Museum. Hudson Yards includes the instantly legendary Vessel, which is the latest and greatest West Side tourist attraction.

Hell's Kitchen used to live up to its ominous name, a name it received for a reason; it was a peripheral place that was not exactly a safe or popular destination. But in recent decades, things have changed, and the neighborhood now proudly wears its name as a badge of honor. The name Hell's Kitchen now means quirky, cool, and even trendy and upscale. The neighborhood is a busy and interesting place that is continually evolving and changing, with rising rents to prove it. Ninth Avenue is a restaurant lover's dream, with a wide array of eateries of every type imaginable. Food is everywhere in Hell's Kitchen, and food generates trash. So does change—old buildings are constantly being demolished and new ones built in their place. Lots of renovation occurs, too. On any given day, hundreds of office, commercial, and residential interiors are gutted and rebuilt. Cranes and bulldozers and dumpsters are everywhere. Commuters bustle, residents shop, workers stroll, and tourists explore. There's a lot happening in Hell's Kitchen all day, every day. This activity generates a great deal of interesting and varied trash of all kinds.

I've been on a trash trajectory for a while now. I've long been interested in the aesthetic of garbage and where and how people discard it. Several of my previous books have covered abandoned places (*Abandoned Queens* and *Abandoned Long Island*, to name two), and a common theme within those abandoned photographs is the trash that has been dumped and strewn about. There was something sadly poetic about the trash, and the abandoned place photographs I took got me thinking: What if I were to take that theme even further and create a book that was an homage to trash? Because pieces of trash are themselves abandoned items, artifacts of our lives. In 2019, I published *Midtown Trash*, which led me to realize I needed to head further west and do a sequel to specifically cover Hell's Kitchen.

What makes this topic especially interesting is that trash is ephemeral. This book is unique in that everything that you see here is long gone. Most of what I photographed was gone within a matter of a day or two, if not hours or even minutes. These images capture something truly fleeting, in many cases intimate momentary portraits of unwanted and unneeded personal effects. There is something poignant and poetic about trash. It's a circle of life kind of thing. Everything you see in this book was once important—needed, wanted, and utilized. Until it wasn't.

All trash is not created equal. There are a few different categories of trash you'll notice in this book.

1) Intentional trash: Junk that was purposely and properly discarded.
2) Reusable trash: The same as above, except it has been thoughtfully exposed and placed so passersby can see, and perhaps take and reuse it, before the trash pickup. File under "one man's trash is another man's treasure."
3) Intentional litter: The garbage that people left behind because they could not be bothered to throw it away properly. This includes trash left on top of closed garbage cans. Littering in New York City is a crime punishable by a fine of at least $75.
4) Fallen litter: Items that were unintentionally dropped, but then left where they fell for someone else to clean. This category most often consists of food or beverage items. It also includes items dropped by young children who may have realized they dropped something, but could not express it in words.
5) Lost items: Items that were unwittingly dropped and either remained where they fell or were picked up and placed somewhere prominent in case the owner returned.

The majority of these photographs were taken between the spring and fall of 2019 on the streets of Hell's Kitchen, mainly between 30th and 50th Streets. The making of a book such as this one could easily turn into a years-long (and hundreds of pages long) documentary project, but I thought it would be more interesting and tell a better story if I contained it to a short, well-defined time frame.

I had one rule when taking these photographs: no interference. I did not pose, move, or touch any of the trash. It is all just as I found it, even though sometimes that meant shadows or unflattering angles. Sometimes closeups worked best to show details of the trash, and other times context was more interesting than the details.

One more thing: I do not intend this book to imply that New York isn't a clean city. It actually is pretty clean, all things considered. Remember that most of the trash in this book was captured in a temporary state of existence, not long before it was swept up or tossed into a truck. Props go to all the men and women who help keep the city streets clean. Also, remember to do your part to help keep New York City clean. Don't litter!

I hope you will enjoy this journey into the world of Hell's Kitchen's trash.

1

Trashy Business

TRASH CAN. Tenth Avenue and 47th Street. Don't litter! Put litter in its place! The trash can itself admonishes us to do the right thing, yet as you will see from many of the images in the book, that seems like a difficult concept for many to grasp.

TRASH EQUIPMENT. Ninth Avenue and 42nd Street. The typical mobile arsenal of the Hudson Yards Hell's Kitchen Alliance cleaning crew member—a trash can, extra trash bags to line the neighborhood cans, and an array of brooms and tools. According to their website, one of the things the HYHK Alliance provides is "supplemental sanitation services" to help keep the sidewalks and streets free from garbage.

FALLEN CAN. Tenth Avenue and 35th Street. Clearly, someone has kicked the can. There's a fine for putting household or business trash in there, but what about for assaulting the can?

TRASH CAN. 34th Street between Eighth and Ninth Avenues. The 34th Street Partnership was launched in 1989. At the time, it was one of New York City's first Business Improvement Districts. It covers a thirty-one-block area centered around 34th Street.

MAN IN CAN. Tenth Avenue and 43rd Street. Trash digging happens a lot, but it's hard to capture someone in the act. Just what are these folks seeking? Could be a newspaper, but more likely cans they can turn in for the five-cent deposit.

TRASH CAN. Ninth Avenue and 44th Street. Every Hell's Kitchen garbage can contains a unique mixture of crap. I see a newspaper (probably one of the free ones), a Starbucks bag, some crumpled aluminum foil, and a brown bag.

TRASH CANS. Ninth Avenue and 49th Street. The ubiquitous trio of cans that can be seen around the city: metal, glass, and plastic recycling; mixed paper recycling; and regular trash.

TRASH MAN. 34th Street between Hudson Boulevard East and Eleventh Avenue. Keeping the area around the Javits Center clean is important because so many people, New Yorkers and visitors alike, attend dozens of expos there every year. While some walk, many take the subway and come out across the street from Javits. A good first impression of the immediate area is critical.

TRASH CAN. Ninth Avenue between 40th and 41st Streets. Keep New York City Beautiful. Hey, stop staring at my imperfections. I'm a trash can; I'm not supposed to be beautiful. I'm the means to keeping the rest of the city beautiful.

TRASH CAN. Ninth Avenue and 34th Street. The trash can as art; the 34th Street Partnership logo has a very retro Art Deco appearance to it, and when seen up close is almost hypnotic.

TRASH CAN. Eleventh Avenue and 44th Street. I find that Tenth and Eleventh Avenues are generally cleaner, probably because they get less foot traffic. More people = more trash.

FENCED TRASH. Tenth Avenue and 47th Street. I prefer my trash to be free range. Caged trash just does not have the same quality of life.

TRASH MAN. Ninth Avenue and 34th Street. A 34th Street Partnership employee at work keeping the eastern edge of Hell's Kitchen clean. Though Hell's Kitchen is often defined as Eighth Avenue and west, the HYHK Alliance defines it as beginning at Ninth Avenue.

▲ **GARBAGE SIGN.** Ninth Avenue and 43rd Street. I love when people put up signs explaining the garbage process. Not sure how one puts boxes on a wall, but maybe there's a trick to it.

▼ **HYHK BAG.** 36th Street between Ninth and Tenth Avenues. Hudson Yard Hell's Kitchen bags are cool. The logo is crisp, and the white bags imply cleanliness.

GARBAGE PLACE SIGN. 38th Street between Eighth and Ninth Avenues. Garbage Place—that has theme park potential.

LOCKED CAN. 34th Street between Eighth and Ninth Avenues. Don't even think about trying to steal this trash can.

TRASH BAGS. 40th Street between Tenth and Eleventh Avenues. A stark reminder of just how much trash a large residential building can generate.

TRASH ON STREET. 41st Street between Ninth and Tenth Avenues. Most of my photographs in this book are relatively close range. This one puts trash more in context of its surroundings. Do you see the four separate trash spots in this image?

TRASH IN FRONT OF DELI. Ninth Avenue and 34th Street. Once this trash is collected, the process will start all over again—more trash will be generated by the folks in the deli and/or the offices or apartments above it, and bagged and brought down curbside to await collection. It's really a never-ending cycle.

RECYCLING SIGNS. 44th Street between Ninth and Tenth Avenues. It was actually helpful to see the Rules of Recycling posted. I'd bet most New Yorkers would benefit from seeing the details spelled out.

DUMPSTER SIGNS. 38th Street between Eighth and Ninth Avenues. If everything in New York had clear rules of engagement like this dumpster, I think we'd all be better off.

DUMPSTER SIGN. 36th Street between Eighth and Ninth Avenues. Police dumpsters are only for the police. Proceed at your own risk!

RUSTY DUMPSTERS. 35th Street between Eighth and Ninth Avenues. Dumpsters come in all sizes, colors, and conditions. A quick paint job and these babies will lose that shabby chic look and be good as new.

DUMPSTERS. Hudson Boulevard East and 36th Street. Four trash-filled dumpsters filled mainly with HYHK trash bags lead me to believe this is a dumping point for the local HYHK Alliance workers who monitor the HYHK cans distributed throughout the neighborhood.

WOOD IN DUMPSTER. 39th Street between Eighth and Ninth Avenues. The amount of residential and commercial construction going on in Hell's Kitchen at any one time is astounding—especially since the neighborhood is continually becoming more gentrified and buildings are being renovated. Dumpsters filled with debris such as this one, loaded with wood, are a common sight.

DUMPSTER DANGER. Ninth Avenue between 36th and 37th Streets. Dumpsters are meant to contain and control large amounts of trash, but beware when walking past one. Sometimes sharp objects protrude from them, and other times, things are precariously balanced. Like a giant version of Jenga, if something inside shifts, another thing could fall.

TRASH TRUCK. 43rd Street between Eighth and Ninth Avenues. A closeup of the rear end of a trash removal truck (aka private carter), and a peek inside.

2

Just Eat It

PIZZA. Ninth Avenue between 39th and 40th Streets. I think fallen New York pizza probably evokes the most sadness in me, of all dropped garbage items. And face-down, no less!

BAGEL AND TWO ROLLS. Ninth Avenue between 45th and 46th Streets. These unfortunate items likely fell from a catering order or a bread delivery to a nearby deli.

SANDWICH. Ninth Avenue between 41st and 42nd Streets. Somebody dropped their peanut butter sandwich! And the bread looks so soft, too. Hopefully some lucky dog came along soon after and had a feast.

FRIED RICE. Tenth Avenue between 44th and 45th Streets. This image really reminds us how even a diligent sanitation worker's broom cannot possibly keep the streets and sidewalks completely clean. Grains of rice on pavement are probably nearly impossible to clean up.

CHIPS. Ninth Avenue between 35th and 36th Streets. New Yorkers spill and drop a lot of food. And there is no ten-second rule for city streets. Once it hits the sidewalk or pavement, that's the end of that.

POTATO FLAKES. 39th Street between Eighth and Ninth Avenues. Three bags and a box of unopened potato flakes. Unopened = usually salvageable. So, I'm not sure what happened here. And besides that, who buys that much potato flakes? Well, perhaps a restaurant or soup kitchen—and a little research reveals that is who the bagged brand caters to. In fact, Hungry Jack is also made by Basic American Foods.

HOT SAUCE. Ninth Avenue and 37th Street. There are numerous eateries on Ninth Avenue and it's not uncommon to see dropped remnants of someone's meal as you walk—whether condiment, napkins, or utensils.

BANANA PEEL. 40th Street and Dyer Avenue. Nobody puts Banana in a corner! Well, usually.

BANANA PEEL. Ninth Avenue and 45th Street. At least this banana peel wound up in a garbage can. Banana peels are the most commonly seen fruit remains in the city, probably because bananas are so easily eaten on the go.

LETTUCE. Ninth Avenue between 37th and 38th Streets. These heads of iceberg must be on their way to the Dead Lettuce Office. New York City sends over a million tons of food waste to landfills every year. Decomposing food waste creates methane, which is a harmful greenhouse gas.

LETTUCE. Ninth Avenue between 48th and 49th Streets. I have a feeling this lettuce stem will not romaine here for very long, what with all the hungry birds in the city.

RASPBERRIES. Ninth Avenue between 45th and 46th Streets. Think about this—if you dropped a bunch of bananas on the street, you'd probably pick them up, because you could still use them. If you dropped a bunch of raspberries, you'd leave them there because there's no salvaging them. But what if the raspberries were in a half-pint container that fell to the ground, would you pick it up? What about an apple? You could still peel it and eat the rest, right?

FOOD BOXES. Ninth Avenue between 40th and 41st Streets. Each of Hell's Kitchen's grocery stores and produce markets toss dozens of cartons every week.

CARDBOARD. Tenth Avenue between 41st and 42nd Streets; 34th Street between Ninth and Tenth Avenues. It's great that NYC recycles now. When I was a kid there was no such thing. Just think of how many thousands of tons of paper and cardboard were just sent to landfills back in the day.

PIECE OF FOOD BOX. Ninth Avenue between 36th and 37th Streets. So much of the street trash we see in the city consists of food and food cartons, or the scraps and remnants thereof.

CHOCOLATE BOX. 47th Street between Eighth and Ninth Avenues. When I tried to go to the website for this chocolate, I got an error message saying the site "took too long to respond." Clearly the site was experiencing happy vibes and could not be disturbed.

RICE KRISPIES TREATS. Ninth Avenue and 38th Street. The real treat is that someone actually bothered to put the empty box into a garbage can.

CANOLA OIL. Ninth Avenue between 37th and 38th Streets. To say that restaurants buy supplies in bulk is no exaggeration, as this 35-pound canola oil container can attest.

PIGEON MEETS PEPPERONI. 43rd Street between Ninth and Tenth Avenues. I watched this pigeon peck and peck at a piece of pepperoni for several minutes, and took twenty-one photos in the process. The pigeon was persistent, but so was I. Birds eat (or attempt to at any rate) much of the food garbage that is out in the open.

PIGEONS EATING. 45th Street and Tenth Avenue. Hungry pigeons are not bothered by curious human onlookers. I think they knew I was not going to try to horn in on their action.

PIGEON AND APPLE. 43rd Street between Ninth and Tenth Avenues. I didn't really see any birds eating garbage in Midtown, but in Hell's Kitchen, it was a feeding frenzy. Here, a pigeon attempts to enjoy an apple core.

SPOON. Eleventh Avenue between 43rd and 44th Streets. "Roadkill trash" is most often soda cans, but can be other unlucky items, such as this flattened metal spoon next to a Burger King bag.

MUDDY PLATE. 43rd Street between Eighth and Ninth Avenues. Rain makes for messy, mucky streets—but also interesting trash photographs. Throw some fallen autumn leaves and building puddle reflections in the mix and you have art(ish).

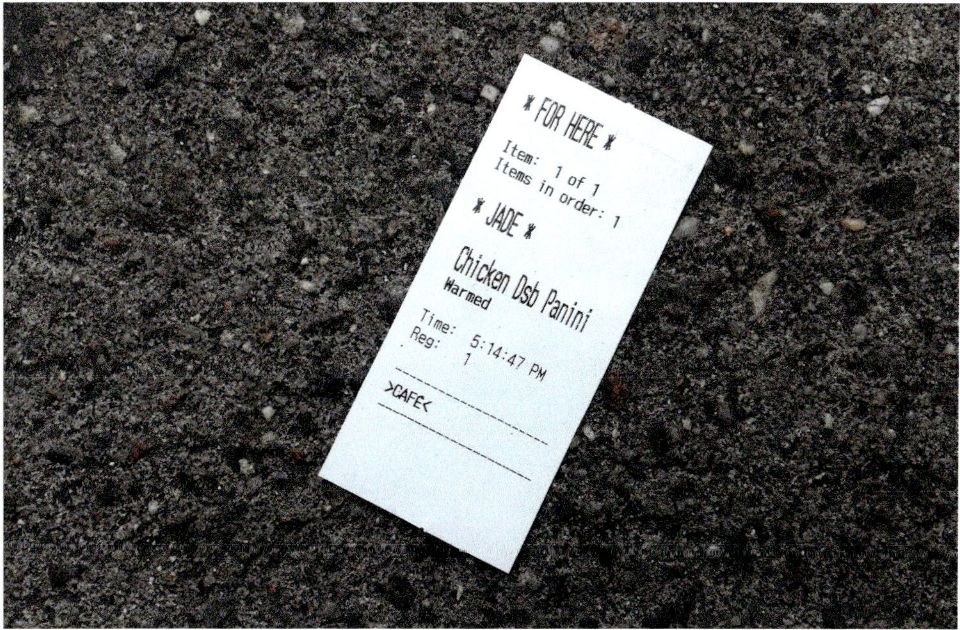

RECEIPT. 34th Street between Eighth and Ninth Avenues. Looks like Jade ordered a warmed chicken panini just after getting off work. Garbage can give us glimpses into the lives of random people, if we care to stop and look.

3

I'll Drink to That

CUP OF LIQUID. Ninth Avenue and 39th Street. Okay, the garbage is literally right next to the cup. Someone took the trouble to bend down and put the cup on the ground rather than toss it into the can? Yes. Yes, they did.

▲ **DRINK ON MAILBOX.** 37th Street between Eighth and Ninth Avenues. People really will leave their trash on any available nearby surface. We'll cling to a cup for an hour, sipping from it, but once we're done, it's like a hot potato.

▼ **CUP.** 37th Street between Eighth and Ninth Avenues. This trash can offered a *trompe l'oeil* situation. When I looked down at this cup partly filled with yellowish liquid, it looked to me like a sunny-side-up egg. See it?

▲ **GRAPE DRINK.** 43rd Street between Tenth and Eleventh Avenues. Can I get a Sac Sac? This Korean drink introduces the concept of "extra pulp" for a grape drink, which seems odd. From reviews I have read, this means whole grapes. Can I get an Eww Eww?

▼ **BOTTLE.** Ninth Avenue between 46th and 47th Streets. Instead of Spin the Bottle, let's play Spot the Bottle. Honestly, garbage often blends in with its surroundings so that unless you look closely, you won't even notice it.

BIG GULP. 35th Street between Eighth and Ninth Avenues. I really feel like people think they are being better than litterers by sticking their trash any place other than the ground.

WINE LIST. 43rd Street between Ninth and Tenth Avenues. These wine lists were tossed by a nearby restaurant. I am eyeing the $109 bottle of Merlot from Duckhorn Vineyards.

CRUSHED CAN. 44th Street between Eighth and Ninth Avenues. Leave an intact soda can out in Manhattan and someone's bound to snatch it up for the five-cent deposit. But once a can is crushed and unredeemable like this one is, it's likely to just lay there for a while.

STARBUCKS CUP. Dyer Avenue between 41st and 42nd Streets. If I can leave my empty cup of water somewhere without having to bend down, then it's even more convenient for me. And it's not littering, right? Wrong!

FLAT CAN. Tenth Avenue and 39th Street. Some enterprising artist could easily collect a bunch of flattened cans and make something from it. I knew an artist named Mr. Imagination who used bottle caps to make sculptures, so why not?

COFFEE CUP. 35th Street between Ninth and Tenth Avenues. A trash illusion. Get your eyes to focus on it and this classic design coffee cup looks as if it's floating above the orange netting.

PYREX AND PLASTIC. 36th Street between Eighth and Ninth Avenues. A glass measuring cup and a two handled plastic Shut Up and Dance cup. Random, yet it somehow makes sense.

COCA COLA CRATE. 42nd Street between Ninth and Tenth Avenues. Catastrophically crushed Coke crate. Crazy cool.

ICE MACHINE. Ninth Avenue between 37th and 38th Streets. The Ice-O-Matic ice machine is used by restaurants and has been made for over fifty years. A new model can range from $1,000-$2,000.

4

What Not to Wear

SHOES ON CAN. 44th Street between Eighth and Ninth Avenues. When footwear is placed atop a trash can, it's an invitation for a passerby to grab themselves a new (to them) pair of shoes.

SHOES. Ninth Avenue between 37th and 38th Streets. Garbage placement sometimes makes me wonder if it's been moved or was left like that to start.

BAG OF SHOES. 47th Street between Eighth and Ninth Avenues. Another instance of someone conspicuously leaving out trash that can potentially be reused. The bag to the left seems to contain flip flops and other items.

SNEAKERS. Ninth Avenue and 42nd Street. Okay, this wins the prize for most innovative place to leave trash—on a fire hydrant. I mean, really, is it that hard to find a trash can? And if the person meant to let someone else find and reuse his Air sneakers, is this really the best place to do so? Oh wait, I guess it is.

SNEAKER AND BOTTLE. 40th Street and Ninth Avenue. The brain wants to make a connection between the bottle and the sneaker (a story involving a drunken night and a painful blister), but maybe they are completely unrelated. If I had to name this image, I'd call it "Shattered Dreams."

BOOTS. Ninth Avenue and 39th Street. This footwear was standing (literally and eerily) next to a garbage can. I mean, I guess it's no different than buying used shoes at a thrift shop, only they're free here.

▲ **CONVERSE BAG.** 36th Street between Eighth and Ninth Avenues. I assume this was from the flagship store on Broadway and Prince Street.

▼ **MASK.** 38th Street between Eighth and Ninth Avenues. This photo was taken six days before Halloween. Boo!

▲ **GREEN GLOVE.** Ninth Avenue between 42nd and 43rd Streets. There's just something so personal and tragic about fallen gloves. I've seen many abandoned sneakers and shoes, but they are mostly intentional leave-behinds. Gloves are almost always single and lost.

▼ **GLOVE.** Ninth Avenue between 35th and 36th Street. A Hell's Kitchen neighborhood sanitation guy saw me photograph this glove, and seconds later, swept it up.

GLOVE. Ninth Avenue and 43rd Street. A Frito-Lay glove? Hmmm. Perhaps formerly worn by a Frito-Lay product delivery person before its untimely loss and death on a sewer grate.

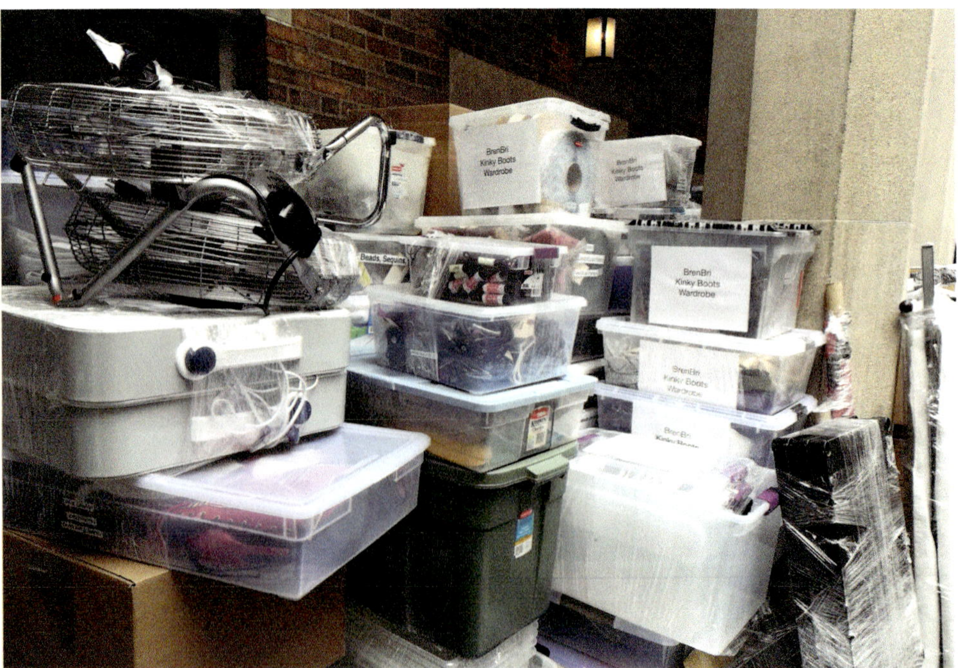

KINKY BOOTS. 45th Street between Eighth and Ninth Avenues. When the famous Broadway musical *Kinky Boots* was about to head out on the road, the props and set pieces were packed up and placed curbside awaiting transport. Not exactly trash, but close enough.

CHILD'S BRACELET. Eighth Avenue between 39th and 40th Streets. In theory, children are always dropping things, but the ratio of lost adult items to lost children's items on city streets is skewed heavily to adults. And yes, I realize that children are not roaming the city streets in packs. But still.

BELT. 43rd Street between Tenth and Eleventh Avenues. Curbside trash is the great randomizer. Trash is quite literally a collection of random unneeded items, and this image presents a leather belt (size medium) along with some clay and plastic pots.

HANGERS. 43rd Street between Ninth and Tenth Avenues. These hangers have been laid out and hung in a very "take me, I'm yours" fashion. It's interesting how some items people feel are deserving of a second chance, while others get tossed into bags and cans where there is no hope of rescue.

PANTS. Ninth Avenue between 45th and 46th Streets. These discarded pants have suffered from some major butt friction. How does that even happen? Ouch!

JACKET. 42nd Street between Eighth and Ninth Avenues. A children's jacket awaits its rightful owner's return on a spring day in Hell's Kitchen.

5

Fully Furnished

CHEST OF DRAWERS. 38th Street between Ninth and Tenth Avenues. Of all the trashed furniture I've seen, this piece was the most aesthetically pleasing to me. It's got a vintage look to it. Those in the know will make the rounds on or just before garbage day to locate and rescue any potential finds in that small window of opportunity before things like this wind up in the jaws of a garbage truck.

BLACK FURNITURE. 38th Street between Ninth and Tenth Avenues. Some trash furniture is in decent shape while other pieces need a little love and hard work to make them usable. It's a judgment call that has to be made on the fly by the trash picker; sometimes it's worth it to just take the piece and decide later, because there is never a guarantee it'll still be there in an hour or two, let alone once the garbage truck comes along.

FOLDED TABLE. 43rd Street between Tenth and Eleventh Avenues. In photos, without their full three dimensionality, objects can sometimes fool the eye into believing they are something else. And this one looks like a giant mouse trap.

DESK. Ninth Avenue between 37th and 38th Streets. You must remember that the most severely damaged of furniture was once shiny and new, and highly functional. This desk likely saw many years of service before it was trashed.

LOCKER. 39th Street between Ninth and Tenth Avenue. Residential trash is often poignant and personal. This children's locker is adorned with colorful letter stickers.

WOOD PANEL. Ninth Avenue and 39th Street. A reminder of just how abstract trash items become when removed from their larger context. I think it's a panel from a kitchen cabinet.

DOOR. 44th Street between Ninth and Tenth Avenues. Sometimes, there is No Exit. Especially when the door has been ripped off its hinges during a construction project.

COUCH. 38th Street between Ninth and Tenth Avenues. Couches are the largest residential trash items you'll see on a city street, other than a bed. Putting a couch out for the garbage seems like such a monumental decision; it'll change the appearance of an entire apartment. Apropos of that —the penultimate episode of the Comedy Central show *Broad City* (a NYC show) featured the main characters jumping into a garbage truck to rescue a couch that was been mistakenly trashed. The pillow from the couch looks like a lost tribble, to reference another television show (*Star Trek*).

RECLINER. Ninth Avenue and 47th Street. It looks like it was beamed directly from someone's living room onto the sidewalk. A little Febreze and it should be good(ish) to go!

CHAIR. 36th Street between Eighth and Ninth Avenues. Sometimes it's the backdrop that's more interesting than the trash itself.

CHAIR. 43rd Street between Eighth and Ninth Avenues. A somewhat vintage chair making puppy dog eyes at me. Apparently, trash knows of my affinity for the vintage and they all hope to be adopted. Word gets around.

RED CHAIR. 43rd Street between Eighth and Ninth Avenues. Before the days of plastic, chairs were made to last for decades. And if a wooden chair broke, it could be salvageable. With plastic chairs, however, damage like this is their end.

FOLDING CHAIR. 43rd Street between Tenth and Eleventh Avenues. At initial glance, this wooden folding chair seems to be in good condition and that may be why it was laid upon the top of the trash bags rather than tucked away out of sight. I do believe that most folks are happy to have others give their discarded possessions a new lease on life.

▲ **WHEELED CHAIR.** 37th Street between Eighth and Ninth Avenues. I had the urge to just push this chair and see how far it would go. But I didn't.

▼ **WHITE CHAIRS.** Ninth Avenue between 37th and 38th Streets. Pairs of chairs can lead to stares. At least from me. The rest of the city just walks right by.

CAR SEATS. Ninth Avenue between 47th and 48th Streets. These seats look to have been ripped out of some kind of vehicle.

MATTRESS. Tenth Avenue between 43rd and 44th Streets. Trashed items take on new, more convenient shapes and sizes once put out on the curb. This mattress has not been placed properly. Per the NYC Department of Sanitation: "Mattresses and Box Springs: Seal these items in a plastic bag before placing them curbside to prevent the spread of bed bugs. Fine Avoided: $100."

MATTRESS. 40th Street between Eighth and Ninth Avenues. This looks like it was a prop in a slasher film (albeit a bloodless one).

PILLOW. 36th Street between Eighth and Ninth Avenues. Colorful trash is eye catching and somehow is more shocking to see being discarded. Out with the boring, in with the fun. Or maybe this pillow is boring compared to its replacement?!

RUG. 43rd Street between Eighth and Ninth Avenues. Rugs are a common trash item and I often just walk right by, but in this case my eye was drawn to the mesmerizing pattern. In fact, as I was writing this caption, I found myself staring at the picture for way too long.

WICKER BASKET. 41st Street between Eighth and Ninth Avenues. You could probably furnish an entire apartment by trash hunting over the course of a few weeks in Hell's Kitchen. While much of the curbside junk is in poor condition, some of it qualifies as "sort of gently used."

TELEVISION. Ninth Avenue between 38th and 39th Streets. According to the Manhattan Borough President's website: "Waste like TVs, cell phones, printers and computers contain hazardous materials like lead and mercury, which can cause serious environmental and health problems when disposed in landfills. Starting January 2015, it is illegal for New Yorkers to discard electronics in the trash—and could lead to a $100 fine."

FRAME AND LAMPS. 46th Street between Eighth and Ninth Avenues. An attractive blue picture frame lies partly trapped under garbage bags, next to a dead lamp. Love the cup placement. Classy addition from a passerby.

6

RANDOM JUNK

PLAYING CARD. Hudson Yards. Clear evidence that someone in Hell's Kitchen is not playing with a full deck. Yeah, I went there.

PLASTIC BAGS. Tenth Avenue between 41st and 42nd Streets. Trash is everywhere. On the ground and even in the air. Stuck in trees, these plastic bags are either unsightly or look like some kind of art installation, depending on your perspective.

PLASTIC BAGS. 42nd Street between Ninth and Tenth Avenues. Another tree-bound bag. Wind carries lighter trash swirling around city streets. Where it winds up is anybody's guess.

EASTER BAG. 44th Street between Eighth and Ninth Avenues. Perhaps it's the touch of sadness implicit in the abandonment or loss of this Easter bag that makes it poignantly sweet. Some items look less commercial and more touching as trash than they might in someone's hand.

BROWN BAG. Eleventh Avenue and 36th Street. Water damaged, this bag lay at a bus stop across the street from the Javits Center. The Sanitation Department collects about 30,000 tons of paper bags per year!

GOLF BAG. 43rd Street between Eighth and Ninth Avenues. You really do see anything and everything put out for the trash. Titleist golf bags are not cheap. This one likely cost $100-200 when new. I have a hunch someone rescued this before it was tossed into the business end of a garbage truck.

KEYS. 43rd Street between Tenth and Eleventh Avenues. It's often the smallest trash that is the most intriguing. These keys have a story. Maybe they were dropped and lost. Maybe they were intentionally tossed. Maybe they open lockers in Grand Central where $10,000 in cash is stashed.

SUCCULENTS. 41st Street between Eighth and Ninth Avenues. One thing that always bothers me is when people throw away living plants. If I had the space, I'd rescue every one of them.

TOOTHBRUSH. 43rd Street and Ninth Avenue. Trash can tell stories, but sometimes it's up to us to create a story. I want to say this toothbrush belonged to an old homeless woman named Debbie, and she accidentally dropped it when she packed up her stuff and moved on to her next temporary encampment.

BRAKE. 44th Street between Ninth and Tenth Avenues. What we have here is a Tektro 160 mm hydraulic bicycle brake rotor.

BICYCLE WHEEL. 44th Street and Tenth Avenue. Something as mundane as a bicycle wheel can look like abstract art in a closeup view. But that's what trash often is anyway—a broken piece, an abstraction of what the original, new item looked like. It's somehow comforting to see trash that is obviously damaged and thus has a reason for being discarded.

RAILROAD TRASH. 45th Street between Tenth and Eleventh Avenues. Trash can be found everywhere, if you look closely enough. More accurately, I think we New Yorkers are just so accustomed to garbage our eyes don't really notice it unless it's been specifically pointed out.

EMPTY LOT. Ninth Avenue between 37th and 38th Streets. Empty lots are practically begging for trash to be dumped, which is one reason why they are usually surrounded by fences. Not that it prevents anyone from tossing in their trash. In this case, anyone in the neighboring apartment building could easily drop junk out the window. Note the fire extinguisher and crushed pot.

TRAFFIC CONE. Ninth Avenue between 33rd and 34th Streets. Traffic cones are used extensively in Manhattan work zones. But occasionally they are crushed by a passing vehicle, *et voila*—trash!

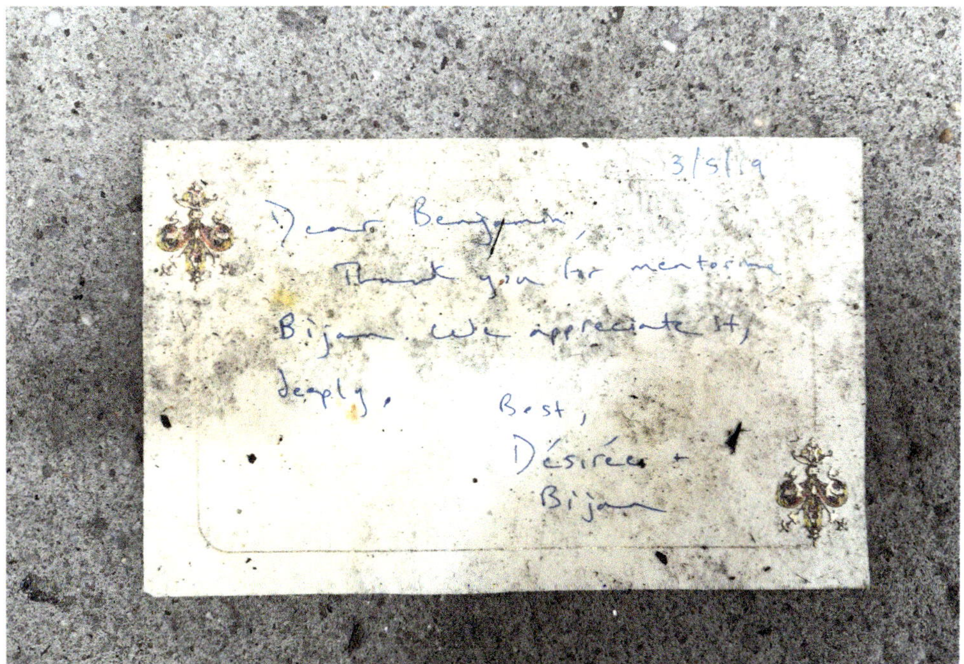

3/5/19

Dear Benjamin,

Thank you for mentoring Bijan. We appreciate it, deeply,

Best,

Désirée + Bijan

NOTE CARD. 46th Street between Ninth and Tenth Avenues. "Dear Benjamin, Thank you for mentoring Bijou. We appreciate it deeply. Best, Desiree + Bijou." Just a guess, but perhaps Benjamin did not appreciate the thank you as deeply as they appreciated him.

FINANCIAL NOTE. 44th Street between Ninth and Tenth Avenues. If you pay attention, you'll see all kinds of papers and notes on the ground in Hell's Kitchen. This looks like some kind of investment to-do list.

NOTE. Ninth Avenue between 39th and 40th Streets. Just an address for a twelve-story building built in 1925 and located between Eighth and Ninth Avenues. One notable tenant as of 2019 is the Elizabeth Foundation for the Arts, which offers space for artists. That's my guess as to why this address was jotted down.

RANDOM TRASH. Ninth Avenue and 43rd Street. A rather disgusting assortment of trash that includes several socks, what appear to be lo mein noodles, metal trays, cigarette butts, and some travel sized bottles.

TARGET BASKET. 34th Street and Ninth Avenue. An escapee from the Target at Herald Square, on 34th Street between Sixth and Seventh Avenues.

▲ **RUBBER BAND.** Ninth Avenue between 45th and 46th Streets. It's not a stretch (yes, intended) to say that there is just so much little trash on the streets and sidewalks of Hell's Kitchen that it's impossible to keep everything clean at all times.

▼ **BALL.** 47th Street between Ninth and Tenth Avenues. Without any context with which to measure scale, this could either be a gumball on a sidewalk, or a soccer ball against a wall. It's the latter. Trash abstraction is all about perspective.

FOAM. 39th Street between Ninth and Tenth Avenues. Trash textures are always interesting, in part because you're often seeing something broken or ripped, exposing the innards of an otherwise uninteresting item.

FLYER. Ninth Avenue and 49th Street. Trash submerged in puddles could be the subject of another book entirely. Water generally makes the city streets messier, and it certainly damages any trash that would have previously been salvageable.

HYDRANT TRASH. 40th Street between Ninth and Tenth Avenues. Fight fire with ... garbage? Like I've said many times, New Yorkers have very strange garbage disposal habits. By the way, see also page 48.

ROAD CONSTRUCTION TRASH. 36th Street between Eighth and Ninth Avenues. Road construction trash and debris is something you'll see a lot of in New York. The City is constantly ripping up pavement to replace water mains or sewer drains. There's a lot of garbage generated by these activities, though sometimes it's not easy to determine if the items are the new waiting to be installed or the old that have been ripped out.

PLASTIC BAG. Ninth Avenue between 35th and 36th Streets. More than 23 billion plastic bags are used in New York State every year! As of March 2020, a new law went into effect mandating that (per the NYS Department of Environmental Conservation web site) "all plastic carryout bags (other than an exempt bag) are banned from distribution by anyone required to collect New York State sales tax."

GRATES. 34th Street between Ninth and Tenth Avenues. Probably the "gratest" trash photo I ever took. Just don't grill me on why I think so.

CIGARETTE PACK. Ninth Avenue and 43rd Street. Empty cigarette packs are among the most common street trash items. Most often they are tossed on the ground, but this one gives an image of someone puffing away on a cigarette while making a phone call.

◀ **FOREIGN CIGARETTES.** 34th Street between Tenth and Eleventh Avenues. The Javits Center draws visitors from all over the world, so I guess I should not be surprised to see this Chinese package of cigarettes.

► **CIGARETTES.** Ninth Avenue between 45th and 46th Streets. Grates such as this one are pretty near impossible to clean, so whatever falls in is likely to stay there for a long time. Aside from cigarettes, if you look closely, you'll see a pencil stub and a little piece of paper that says, "Thank You."

RANDOM TRASH. 39th Street between Eighth and Ninth Avenues. This must be the most eclectic assortment of garbage I've seen in Hell's Kitchen. A bracelet, a travel size bottle of shampoo, four butter pats, a Big Gulp cup, and a key.

GUITAR CASE. 39th Street between Eighth and Ninth Avenues. Every single piece of trash has a story to tell, but some stories are more mysterious and compelling than others. An abandoned guitar case leaves much to the imagination. Perhaps a street performer was ousted from her spot in a hurry and left the case behind?

BATTERY. 45th Street between Ninth and Tenth Avenues. This battery should charge someone with battery, because it's clearly been battered. Sorry, I had to.

▲ BAG OF SHREDS. Tenth Avenue between 44th and 45th Streets. According to a Department of Sanitation report, in 2017, 17% of all residential curbside trash was paper and cardboard (recyclable).

▼ SHREDDED PAPER. 36th Street between Eighth and Ninth Avenues. Zooming in on trash can make for dramatic and often abstract images.

MOP. Eighth Avenue between 39th and 40th Streets. This mop is perfectly camouflaged to match the color of the sidewalk, and trick unsuspecting debris. Now the tables are turned and it is trash itself, and hoping that it escapes its fate unseen.

PRINTER CARTRIDGE. 39th Street between Eighth and Ninth Avenues. This discarded piece of equipment sits in a puddle which reflects the image of perhaps the very building in which it was used.

RANDOM TRASH. 35th Street between Tenth and Eleventh Avenues. A small cluster of assorted paper and plastic trash with a weed growing from its midst.

UMBRELLA. 46th Street between Ninth and Tenth Avenues. A broken umbrella is useless and unwieldy. Most New Yorkers drop them on the spot whether or not there's a trash can in sight.

PARKING TICKET. Ninth Avenue between 45th and 46th Streets. Parking tickets are usually secured under a windshield wiper, so chances are good that those tickets on the ground have been tossed there by their recipients.

FOAM AND LUGGAGE. 41st Street between Tenth and Eleventh Avenues. Too big to bag, luggage is a common curbside sight. And pretty much all the items of luggage I've seen were in poor (or dirty) condition. People tend to hang on to suitcases until the bitter end.

PHONES. 48th Street between Eighth and Ninth Avenues. These dead office telephones were about to be tossed into the back of a junk removal truck.

TREE BRANCHES. Ninth Avenue and 45th Street. Looks like these were trimmed from a nearby flowering springtime tree. I think it looks nice. I'd recommend that every trash can get its own sprig of green and pink!

TIRE. Ninth Avenue between 36th and 37th Streets. A piece of a dead Goodyear G159 tire, made mainly for lower speed delivery vehicles.

STOP SIGN. Ninth Avenue between 35th and 36th Streets. Everything eventually becomes trash, even the things we'd never imagine being discarded. Everything stops being useful at some point.

CONSTRUCTION TRASH. 43rd Street between Tenth and Eleventh Avenues. There is an incredible amount of construction going on in the city at any given time. A listing of NYC building permits for just the month of April 2017, is 2,500 pages long!

PINK LUGGAGE. 35th Street between Eighth and Ninth Avenues. I do not condone trash violence. But what happens in the dumpster, stays in the dumpster.

BROOM. 43rd Street between Eighth and Ninth Avenues. Even the very tools that help clean up the streets of Hell's Kitchen themselves become trash when they're worn ragged. The song "Dust in the Wind" popped in my head while writing this caption.

EMPTY BOX. 41st Street between Eighth and Ninth Avenues. And on that note, I will end this book. Until the next book: Good night.